MONEY TALKS

WRITTEN BY JEFF PRIES

THOMAS NELSON
Since 1798

NASHVILLE   DALLAS   MEXICO CITY   RIO DE JANEIRO   BEIJING

Printed in China.
08 09 10 11 12 SS 9 8 7 6 5 4 3 2 1

■■■ CONTENTS

Introduction 4

Chapter 1: Investments 8
Chapter 2: Stuff 24
Chapter 3: Leverage 40
Chapter 4: Charity 56
Chapter 5: Priorities 70

Leader's Guide 86
Leader's Guide Chapter 1: Investments 91
Leader's Guide Chapter 2: Stuff 95
Leader's Guide Chapter 3: Leverage 100
Leader's Guide Chapter 4: Charity 103
Leader's Guide Chapter 5: Priorities 106

■■ INTRODUCTION

LIQUID

Five episodes. One story.

God's Word is as true today as it was when it was written.

But for too long, we have looked at God's Word and wondered how it could possibly impact our lives. It's one thing to simply read the Bible. It's something different altogether to understand it. Far too often we read these stories about people in an ancient land, and we're left feeling flat. "What's this got to do with me?" We know in our hearts that what we're reading is true, right, and good, but we can't see any real way to apply it.

That's where *LIQUID* comes in.

LIQUID presents true-to-life stories of characters with real problems. Because what's the point in putting together a study of God's Word that doesn't deal with any of the issues we actually face? Along with each chapter in this book is a film, filled with characters who live in our world—the real world. Yet their problems and struggles mirror the same struggles found in stories in the Bible.

Jesus is the master storyteller. He helped people understand, made them contemplate, made them consider. He wasn't afraid to cut a story a couple of ways, as if he was saying, "Let me say it another way, a different way, so you can understand." He often gave answers by asking questions in return, so people would investigate, think, learn. It's how he did it, so it's why we do it. We translate ancient stories into the language of today's culture, and we ask relevant questions to help you discover the truth for yourself.

Whether you're with a small group, or simply by yourself, all we ask is that you take a deep breath, pop in the DVD, and then read through these pages and think carefully about the questions and the Scriptures. These are not questions from the SAT—they don't have definitive answers. They are designed for you to reflect upon based on your perspective. Everyone's discoveries will be different. But that's what's great about God's truth—it's one truth, but it's formed differently around each person.

It's simply about taking in, reflecting, and coming up with something useful for your life. Now at last we have an immediate, portable, relevant way to experience God's Word. A revolutionary new way to study the Bible.

LIQUID. God's Word flowing through your life.

▰▰ MONEY TALKS

Money is a sticky subject. No one likes talking about it, much less figuring out how they can be better with it. But if you think you have ever had issues with money, you should meet the Penders. While money is a part of all of our lives—the struggles of how much is enough, what to give, when to give, when does need become want—to the Pender family, money is everything.

If you are holding this book, you are about to embark on a five-week study of stewardship. You're probably thinking, *What does stewardship even mean, and why would I want to get better at it?* Basically stewardship is all about how we use the resources we've been given. (A little tip: it should usually be *opposite* of the way the Penders use it!) *Money Talks* reviews four passages from Christ's teaching about the relationship between giving and God (The Parable of the Barns, The Parable of the Shrewd Manager, The Parable of the Talents, The Rich Young Ruler), as well as Paul's thoughts on the beauty of giving (2 Corinthians 9).

These biblical passages are paralleled by a comedy (yes, a comedy) about a dysfunctional Orange County, California, family's struggles with their unending wealth and ever-elusive happiness. Shot in the "mockumentary" style, which has elevated such shows and films as "The Office" or "Best in Show," *Money Talks* gives us a chance to take a lighthearted look at one of the more difficult issues in our faith: stewardship.

CHAPTER 1: INVESTMENTS

Liquid

Growing up, I had a bunch of important relationships. My father was an important figure in my life, and I had a lot of great friends. Oh yeah, and I can't leave God out of the equation. But if I was to be totally honest, as a guy growing up, I would have chosen a girl over anything else any day. When someone I was interested in liked me, I was on top of the world. When I felt rejected or dumped by the opposite sex, life wasn't even worth living. I guess you could say my most important relationship could have been with my dad, or maybe even God, but instead it usually came down to a girl.

Growing up, what was your most important relationship?

Play video episode now.

It's so easy to spend a hundred dollars these days. A good meal, a couple of tickets to the ball game, a great outfit—buy any of these things and you've dropped at least that much. But investing a hundred dollars, that's a little more interesting. What could I do that would bring a return? It would have to be a return that didn't benefit myself, or I'd feel too guilty. I got it! I could get something for my wife. But it couldn't be something like flowers, she'd get suspicious and think I did something wrong. Maybe I could get her a hair appointment at a fancy salon. But then she might think I don't like her hairstyle. I guess spending one hundred dollars isn't as easy as it seems.

What were all the ways the characters invested their money? What was their motivation?

What would you say each character's relationship with James is like? How did that impact the way each of them participated?

[14] "The kingdom of heaven is like a man who was going to another place for a visit. Before he left, he called for his servants and told them to take care of his things while he was gone. [15] He gave one servant five bags of gold, another servant two bags of gold, and a third servant one bag of gold, to each one as much as he could handle. Then he left. [16] The servant who got five bags went quickly to invest the money and earned five more bags. [17] In the same way, the servant who had two bags invested them and earned two more. [18] But the servant who got one bag went out and dug a hole in the ground and hid the master's money.

[19] "After a long time the master came home and asked the servants what they did with his money. [20] The servant who was given five bags of gold brought five more bags to the master and said, 'Master, you trusted me to care for five bags of gold, so I used your five bags to earn five more.' [21] The master answered, 'You did well. You are a good and loyal servant. Because you were loyal with small things, I will let you care for much greater things. Come and share my joy with me.'

[22] "Then the servant who had been given two bags of gold came to the master and said, 'Master, you gave me two bags of gold to care for, so I used your two bags to earn two more.'

23 The master answered, 'You did well. You are a good and loyal servant. Because you were loyal with small things, I will let you care for much greater things. Come and share my joy with me.'

24 "Then the servant who had been given one bag of gold came to the master and said, 'Master, I knew that you were a hard man. You harvest things you did not plant. You gather crops where you did not sow any seed. 25 So I was afraid and went and hid your money in the ground. Here is your bag of gold.' 26 The master answered, 'You are a wicked and lazy servant! You say you knew that I harvest things I did not plant and that I gather crops where I did not sow any seed. 27 So you should have put my gold in the bank. Then, when I came home, I would have received my gold back with interest.'

28 "So the master told his other servants, 'Take the bag of gold from that servant and give it to the servant who has ten bags of gold. 29 Those who have much will get more, and they will have much more than they need. But those who do not have much will have everything taken away from them.' 30 Then the master said, 'Throw that useless servant outside, into the darkness where people will cry and grind their teeth with pain.'"

What do you learn about the master and each of the servants?

What do the actions and responses of the master and each of the servants say about how they view their relationship with each other?

his audience—that of a landowner entrusting his fortune to financial stewards, or accountants. Sometimes they would be hired employees, or, as was the case in this parable, they could also be servants.

At the time Jesus told this story, the talent (the denomination of money used in several Bible translations) would have been worth approximately several thousand denaraii. One denarius was worth a full day's pay for these servants, so one talent would be worth many years' worth of wages. Some estimates put the value at three hundred thousand dollars in today's currency. So the bags of money that the landowner gave to the servants for investing were significant sums of money, even the one with one denarius (coin).

One common practice (albeit not very profitable) was to bury one's money for safekeeping. In fact, some of those buried, forgotten, or left-behind treasures are still being found today. However, the most common investment with low risk was to deposit money into a savings account for a nominal cost or interest.

Doubling one's money by investing it in various ways was commonplace and would have been the expectation of the landowner. Although there were risks involved in investing, the risks were minimal, and a landowner would have entrusted these sums of money to someone in the marketplace who was trustworthy and shrewd and had shown previous success with investments.

I was a 1984 first round pick of the New York Yankees. God had blessed me with a golden arm that allowed me to throw the ball really hard. The Yankees blessed me with a good chunk of money. I would love to say I took the money and sent a handful of underprivileged kids to camp, or helped out a church that was struggling and needed financial assistance—but that wouldn't be true. What did I do? I made the bright decision to invest a good portion of my money in a brand-new Porsche. Faithful stewardship? I don't think so. The only thing I had faith in was that this money from the Yankees was just the first of many millions. I was wrong. What does unfaithful stewardship look like? In this case, it looked shiny and cool and all about me. It was a textbook case of selfishness.

God entrusts everyone with money and resources. What does faithful and unfaithful stewardship look like?

How might that reflect a person's relationship with God?

I don't have an endless amount of resources. Actually, I don't know why I wrote *resources* when what I mean is *money*. I don't have a ton of money. My family and I do okay, we get by. But what I try to do is take what we do have and use it to bless others. We try to help with the church, people overseas, those who are struggling. The reality is, our giving isn't based on an overabundance of money. My wife and I don't look at our bank account and wonder what we are going to do with all the extra cash. We give because we love God. We look at all he's given us—family, kids, friends—and we feel close to him. There have been times in my life when I've had money, but I didn't feel close to God and the thought of giving to him or others never crossed my mind. Does your relationship with God influence your spending habits? It definitely did mine.

How does your relationship with God affect the ways you use the money and resources God has given you?

What relational changes will you make to help improve your stewardship?

Every summer the senior pastor of our church goes away and entrusts me with most of the summer series and a big slice of the teaching. I just want to do a great job and use the gifts and talents God has given me to bless others. If I'm honest I have to admit that there's a small part of me that wants to do a good job, probably because I want to be liked by people. But the biggest reason I want to do a good job is to bless our senior pastor, to give him the freedom to take a much-needed break and know that things back home are going to be OK. Do I love to preach? No. It's nerve-racking for me. I do it, not because I have to, not because I want to, but because I care about the senior pastor. It comes down to a relationship. That's my motivation.

How has your relationship with God in the past affected the way you handle your money and resources?

How have you been a good steward with God's provision? What are ways you have not been a good steward?

Why do you feel like peoples' relationships with God have such an impact on stewardship?

Who is someone you know who seems to handle the resources God has given them the correct way? What are the things that help him or her be a good steward?

How has God blessed you? What are specific steps you can take to bless him and others?

Are there things that keep you from being a good steward? What are they?

CHAPTER 2: STUFF

Liquid

What makes a relationship satisfying? Well, I know most people are going to say trust, so I guess I can say that. But I'm a little hesitant to go along with the crowd. After all, if I was going to shoot straight, I might have to say that looks are important too. You have to be attracted to someone, right? Then I think about fun. After all, if you're not having fun then it can turn into a real drag. But I hate even writing that. It makes me feel like one of the guys who only care about the surface stuff. Now that I think about it, maybe trust really is an important part of a satisfying relationship. Because the reality is, below all of the stuff that looks good on the outside, if you are going to be satisfied in a relationship, you need to be able to say, "I will come through for you, and I need you to come through for me." Simply put, we all need trust.

For you, what are the most important aspects of a satisfying relationship?

Play video episode now.

We watch James and we laugh. After all, he is an eccentric fool at times. Sure, James is different from us, but is he really that different? OK, yes, he really is that different, but I can still find myself struggling with the same things he deals with. He wants more, he looks for ways to one-up someone, he feels insecure. I know I don't have enough fingers to count the number of times I have left a friend's house that is bigger and nicer than mine, a place that makes me feel small and insignificant, and I have thought, *I've got nothing*. Wouldn't it be nice if I could always drive away saying to myself, *I'm OK! I have God and he is enough!* That's a nice concept, but I'm sad to say I don't always feel it.

In this episode, what are all of the things in which James puts his trust?

Why do you think he keeps making the same mistake over and over again?

¹³ Someone in the crowd said to Jesus, "Teacher, tell my brother to divide with me the property our father left us."

¹⁴ But Jesus said to him, "Who said I should judge or decide between you?" ¹⁵ Then Jesus said to them, "Be careful and guard against all kinds of greed. Life is not measured by how much one owns."

¹⁶ Then Jesus told this story: "There was a rich man who had some land, which grew a good crop. ¹⁷ He thought to himself, 'What will I do? I have no place to keep all my crops.' ¹⁸ Then he said, 'This is what I will do: I will tear down my barns and build bigger ones, and there I will store all my grain and other goods. ¹⁹ Then I can say to myself, "I have enough good things stored to last for many years. Rest, eat, drink, and enjoy life!"

²⁰ "But God said to him, 'Foolish man! Tonight your life will be taken from you. So who will get those things you have prepared for yourself?'

²¹ "This is how it will be for those who store up things for themselves and are not rich toward God."

²² Jesus said to his followers, "So I tell you, don't worry about the food you need to live, or about the clothes you need for your body. ²³ Life is more than food, and the body is more than clothes. ²⁴ Look at the birds. They don't

plant or harvest, they don't have storerooms or barns, but God feeds them. And you are worth much more than birds. [25] You cannot add any time to your life by worrying about it. [26] If you cannot do even the little things, then why worry about the big things? [27] Consider how the lilies grow; they don't work or make clothes for themselves. But I tell you that even Solomon with his riches was not dressed as beautifully as one of these flowers. [28] God clothes the grass in the field, which is alive today but tomorrow is thrown into the fire. So how much more will God clothe you? Don't have so little faith! [29] Don't always think about what you will eat or what you will drink, and don't keep worrying. [30] All the people in the world are trying to get these things, and your Father knows you need them. [31] But seek God's kingdom, and all the other things you need will be given to you.

[32] "Don't fear, little flock, because your Father wants to give you the kingdom. [33] Sell your possessions and give to the poor. Get for yourselves purses that will not wear out, the treasure in heaven that never runs out, where thieves can't steal and moths can't destroy. [34] Your heart will be where your treasure is."

What were the man in the crowd and the man with the barns concerned about?

What was Jesus' response, and what were his concerns for them?

CULTURAL AND HISTORICAL THOUGHTS:
Jesus had been preaching on hypocrisy, hell, and unforgivable sin when a person from the crowd yelled a question to him—one that was completely out of context and instantly revealed the man's heart. He was not there to learn from Jesus, but rather to use Jesus for his own selfish results—increasing his inheritance.

Jewish tradition and culture dictated the way an inheritance was to be divided and left very little open for deliberation. In those days the estate was divided among sons only. Women would benefit from their husband's estate, not from their father's. The oldest son would always get twice as much as any of the other sons. So if there were only two sons, as appears to be the case here, noted in the first part of the passage, the estate would have been split into thirds, with two-thirds going to the older son and one-third to the youngest.

Jesus continues his teaching on greed by describing a successful harvester whose yields are so great his barns won't hold them. So he builds bigger barns. The tie here is where one moves from provision to greed and anxiety about having enough. The history of the Jewish community speaks of not only prayer and fasting but charity. Leviticus 19:9–10 says, "When you harvest your crops on your land, do not harvest all the way to the corners of your fields. If grain falls onto the ground, don't gather it up. Don't pick all the grapes in your vineyards, and don't pick up the grapes that fall to the ground. You must leave those things for poor people and for people traveling through your country." The early Christian community was called to continue this caring for the neighbor.

I'm staring at a twenty dollar bill. I am intrigued by the words on the back side: "In God We Trust." It seems ironic to me that the two powers that I trust in the most are printed on the same piece of paper. As I look at it, I ask myself, *If I were to trust in just one, either the twenty dollar bill or God, which would it be?* Staring at the two best gods I know, which one am I willing to make number one? As always, it depends on when you ask me. The value of the words, "In God We Trust," means everything to me, but the value of the currency keeps calling my name. It's a cyclical dilemma. Once I finally think I'm free from the call of money, it always finds a way to reprioritize itself in my life.

If there were a scale of trust with money on one side and God on the other, where would you put the two men in the story?

Money —|——|——|——|——|——|——|——|——|— God

What might move them in one direction or the other?

What are the consequences of putting trust in money? In God?

When I started dating my wife, we hit it off right from the start. We enjoyed the same things, liked to laugh and enjoy life, loved God, and most importantly, she loved to watch sports. Problem was, when we met, I was waiting tables in a restaurant as I finished up my schooling. Every now and then she would look at me with that look of, "You're going to be more than a waiter, aren't you?" You know the whole "you're a good guy, so please tell me you're not a total loser" look. I really wanted to tell her, "Don't worry, I will take care of you. I will do whatever it takes. You sign up with me, and I am all for you." God says the same things, but more poetically, with more power and authority than I could ever pull off. But just like I meant it when I said it to my wife, God means it just the same. He says, "Trust me."

Using the scale below, where would you place yourself? How will your mind-set and actions have to change to move you closer to God?

Money ———|———|———|———|———|———|———|———|——— God

What will be the good and bad consequences of making that change?

I just waved good-bye to my son. It was the first time I ever let him go somewhere on a Friday night with a bunch of high school kids driving. It actually scared me to death. I was on the verge of pulling him out of the car and telling him that I would take him, but I didn't. What am I going to do, drive him around for the rest of his life? And then I mumbled something to myself that surprised me. I said, "I guess I have to trust God." And there you have it: all the money in the world won't protect my kid when he's off on his own with his friends. I have to let go and trust God. I learned a small lesson that night, but can I apply it to all areas of my life?

What makes money something in which we desire to put our trust?

What are the things in life that have helped you trust in God more than money?

What are things that have led you to trust in money more than God?

What is the advantage of trusting in God over money, and vice versa?

CHAPTER 3: LEVERAGE

Liquid

When I was fourteen years old, I had a moped——you know, the little motorcycle with the bicycle pedals. Sure, it was no Harley, but at fourteen I was the coolest kid in eighth grade. Why? Because I was free, independent, and didn't need any more rides from Mom and Dad. This kid had wheels! Back then, I couldn't believe they bought it for me. It was a lot of cash and kind of dangerous. But now that I look back, I don't think it was only me looking for freedom. I think Mom and Dad were looking for the same thing.

What was the first expensive thing you ever owned?

Play video episode now.

[1] Jesus told this story to his disciples: "A rich man hired a manager to handle his affairs, but soon a rumor went around that the manager was thoroughly dishonest. [2] So his employer called him in and said, 'What's this I hear about your stealing from me? Get your report in order, because you are going to be dismissed.'

[3] "The manager thought to himself, 'Now what? I'm through here, and I don't have the strength to go out and dig ditches, and I'm too proud to beg. [4] I know just the thing! And then I'll have plenty of friends to take care of me when I leave!'

[5] "So he invited each person who owed money to his employer to come and discuss the situation. He asked the first one, 'How much do you owe him?' [6] The man replied, 'I owe him eight hundred gallons of olive oil.' So the manager told him, 'Tear up that bill and write another one for four hundred gallons.'

[7] "'And how much do you owe my employer?' he asked the next man. 'A thousand bushels of wheat,' was the reply. 'Here,' the manager said, 'take your bill and replace it with one for only eight hundred bushels.'

[8] "The rich man had to admire the dishonest rascal for being so shrewd. And it is true that the citizens of this world are more shrewd than the godly are.

[9] "I tell you, use your worldly resources to benefit others and make friends. In this way, your generosity stores up a reward for you in heaven."

What did the rich man and the manager want, and what did they do to get it?

What did Jesus want the disciples to learn from the story?

CULTURAL AND HISTORICAL THOUGHTS:

The meaning of this parable is straightforward enough, and is provided by Jesus himself—"use your worldly resources to benefit others and make friends," with the additional application of using advantages in this world to gain for yourself favor in the next. This additional application was embraced by most early church writers, as evidenced by the following quote from Asterius of Amasea: "When, therefore, any one anticipating his end and his removal to the next world, lightens the burden of his sins by good deeds, either by canceling the obligations of debtors, or by supplying the poor with abundance, by giving what belongs to the Lord, he gains many friends, who will attest his goodness before the Judge, and secure him by their testimony a place of happiness."

A hired financial steward (money manager or accountant) in that culture had the cultural right to forgive debts. One theory is that the steward simply forgave a portion of the debt to win friends who would take care of him when he became unemployed. A second theory is that he had put a commission on the original bill and that he had in fact just cut the commission for the purpose of gaining friends who would help him later.

The New Jerusalem Bible states, "It was the custom for a steward, or responsible servant, to take commission on all sales of his master's goods. This was his only means of making a salary. In the present case the original loan was presumably fifty measures (four hundred gallons in the translation above) of olive oil and eighty measures (eight hundred bushels in the translation above) of wheat. In reducing the debtors' bills, he is not depriving his master of anything, but only sacrificing his own immediate interests by forgoing his legitimate commission. It is for this that he is praised as 'astute.'"

Regardless of his methods, it should be noted that Jesus "commends the dishonest manager for his shrewdness, not the shrewd manager for his dishonesty." [1]

1. Henry Wansbrough, ed., *The New Jerusalem Bible* (New York; London: Doubleday; Darton, Longman & Todd, 1985).

I'm driving my boys around in a Suburban filled with their friends—about eight kids in all. They start making fun of my car because it has crank-down windows. Kids nowadays have never seen them before. My kids are embarrassed, and I start feeling like a loser. They ask what I do for work and my kids inform them that I'm a pastor. I hear another chuckle from the backseat. If I was a warship, that little chuckle was the final hit. I am starting to take on water, and I am sinking fast. And then I see a donut shop—an opportunity for me to restore my pride and status in the eyes of the kids. When I buy the boys a couple of dozen donuts, I go from laughing-stock to hero for the relatively small investment of twenty dollars. But this is what I'm thinking: I want them to see that pastors can be fun, too, even if they drive a beat-up Suburban. If they think pastors are cool, maybe they'll think church isn't so bad either. And then maybe they'll think Jesus is alright, too. So maybe it's a little bit of a stretch, but then again, that twenty dollars might make an eternal difference someday.

What are ways people use money today to gain friends and influence people?

In the same way, how do people use their resources to produce eternal benefits?

The greatest, most over-the-top day comes around for me twice a year. I wake up at 5:30 in the morning, drive to Palm Springs along with twenty-five other pastors, and play thirty-six holes of golf on one of the best courses in the area. We finish the day with dinner at Wally's, a what-am-I-doing-at-such-a-nice-restaurant kind of place. I know what you're thinking: How are we pastors able to afford all of this? Aren't we supposed to be suffering for Jesus? One generous man is to thank. He wants to pour into our lives and give us the kind of day that will pump us up and keep us going. What a guy, a true friend. He wants to make a difference in our lives, and in return, he hopes that we'll make a difference in the lives of others.

How does using money to make friends look different from using money to point people to God?

What are ways you have used money for eternal purposes? How did it make you feel?

What was a time you missed an opportunity to use your money for eternal purposes instead of personal gain? How do you wish you would have acted?

CHAPTER 4: CHARITY

Yesterday, out of the blue, I get a call from someone who had four tickets to the Anaheim Ducks hockey game that he wanted me to have. I said, "Great!" Who wouldn't want to see the Stanley Cup champions play? When I picked up the tickets, I caught a glimpse of the price: $185 a ticket. Are you kidding me? I was holding four of them. Four tickets that make up about half of my mortgage payment! So I take a buddy and my two young boys. We get to the game and we are sitting right on the glass! During the second period, the referee motions to my boys to open the hole in the glass for photographers, and hands them each a puck. Was this person generous to give us the tickets? You bet. Even over-the-top? No doubt. I have a ticket stub, and two pucks to prove it.

Describe a time when someone was over-the-top generous to you.

Play video episode now.

Poor James. All he wants to do is bless his family. After all, what is more giving than Christmas? So even if it is July, there's nothing wrong with spreading a little good cheer twice a year. But the closest people in his life shut him down, and he's faced with a lonely walk on the beach . . . a walk where he finds even more opportunity to give. Three guys in need of a miracle. He gives them food, a place to live, and even makes a record deal with them. Unfortunately he ticks off his wife in the process. I guess he can't get everything right. When we give, God continues to open up opportunities to give more. We feel blessed when we give, which is why giving feels so good. Every time we give, God gives us a little gift—the opportunity and means to give again.

What are all of the ways James gives in the film?

What are the things he experiences by giving?

[6] Remember this: The person who plants a little will have a small harvest, but the person who plants a lot will have a big harvest. [7] Each one should give as you have decided in your heart to give. You should not be sad when you give, and you should not give because you feel forced to give. God loves the person who gives happily. [8] And God can give you more blessings than you need. Then you will always have plenty of everything—enough to give to every good work. [9] It is written in the Scriptures:

> "He gives freely to the poor.
>> The things he does are right and will continue forever." — Psalm 112:9

[10] God is the One who gives seed to the farmer and bread for food. He will give you all the seed you need and make it grow so there will be a great harvest from your goodness. [11] He will make you rich in every way so that you can always give freely. And your giving through us will cause many to give thanks to God. [12] This service you do not only helps the needs of God's people, it also brings many more thanks to God. [13] It is a proof of your faith. Many people will praise God because you obey the Good News of Christ—the gospel you say you believe—and because you freely share with them and with all others. [14] And when they pray, they will wish they could be with you because of the great grace that God has given you. [15] Thanks be to God for his gift that is too wonderful for words.

What do you learn about the cause and effect of giving: for God, the giver, and the receiver?

CULTURAL AND HISTORICAL THOUGHTS:

In 1 Corinthians, Paul used strong words to set them on the right path and instruct them in their Christian walks. Most of the church had responded in the right spirit, however some were denying Paul's authority and questioning his motives.

Paul wrote 2 Corinthians at Philippi, or, as some think, Thessalonica, early in the year AD 58, and was sent to Corinth by Titus. In this letter he addresses not only the church in Corinth, but also the saints in Athens, Cenchrea, and other cities in Greece. Paul spends the first eight chapters defending his position in the church as well as his relationship to them and his intentions.

Beginning in chapter nine, Paul provides the longest sustained writing on giving, addressing motives, priorities, and principles for Christian giving to the widows, disabled, and marginalized. Paul had previously organized a collection of funds for the poor in the Jerusalem church. Many of the churches had committed to participate in this fund, and Paul was urging the Corinthians to follow through on their previous commitment.

When talking about giving generously, Paul uses imagery with which his audience would immediately identify—planting and harvesting crops. They understood that if they planted little they would reap little, and they knew if they planted with a generous amount of seed they would reap a plentiful harvest.

It's an easy myth to buy into. Everyone wants to believe that all you have to do is give and God will give you even more money. I have to admit, I've bought into that idea before. It's kind of like turning God into a slot machine. You put some coins in and hopefully get more back. It never felt right, but it was an easy way to view giving, hoping to get something better back each time. Now when I think back on that mentality, I realize it was so selfish. I was trying to manipulate God. I know better now. I still give, but I do it to help others out, not to see what I can get. It's a much more fulfilling way to live.

What are some of the ways the world views giving? What are ways that Christians view giving? Compare and contrast your answers.

How do the views align or differ from the truths of the passage we just read?

Last year I led a group of young couples down to Mexico to build houses. We built two houses for two needy families. Both families' houses had been made of cardboard and plywood and sheltered about seven people each. Each house we built cost five thousand dollars. Ten thousand dollars is a lot of money for young couples just starting out, but they committed themselves to raising all of it. They sent out letters to family and friends and prayed that the money would come in. We were leaving in two weeks. Would we make our goal? Would people give? We left for Mexico with eight thousand dollars in the bank, hoping the other two thousand would come when we got back. When we came back, people kept giving and we made it by two hundred dollars. People gave, people were blessed, people took a step. We're heading back down soon to build another house. I checked the account today to see if there was any more money that could be used for other houses, and there was ten thousand dollars sitting in there. I was amazed. When we're generous, when we use our time, our talents, and our money, God comes through with more so we can keep giving again and again.

What principles from the passage have changed your view on giving? How may these principles influence your giving in the future?

What is an area in your life where you feel called to give? What is a step you can take to give in this area?

I will never forget the first time I went to the church where I work now. I was twelve years old. The thing that stuck out to me the most is that they didn't pass an offering plate, but had offering boxes in the back of the church. I missed the plate passing, and not because I was looking for a chance to sneak a couple of bucks. I missed it because it was probably the only part of the service I really got—the concept of God blessing us, and us giving back to him. Now that I am grown up, I like having the boxes in the back, especially as a pastor at the church. It makes me feel like we aren't forcing church members to drop something in when it comes by. People do it out of their own desire. Giving back to God while at the same time receiving a blessing—concepts I already knew, even when I was twelve years old.

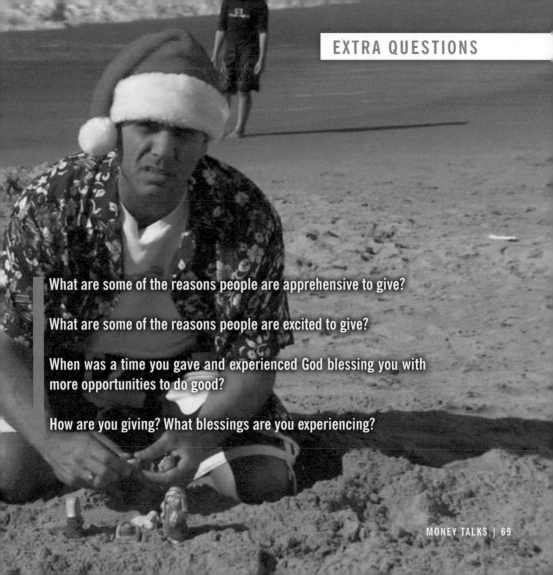

What are some of the reasons people are apprehensive to give?

What are some of the reasons people are excited to give?

When was a time you gave and experienced God blessing you with more opportunities to do good?

How are you giving? What blessings are you experiencing?

CHAPTER 5: PRIORITIES

I love my fifty-two-inch, high-definition, surround-sound plasma TV. I love sitting in front of it after a long day and just zoning out. I love inviting friends over to watch the game. I love distracting my kids with a movie so I can get a few minutes of peace and quiet. My TV is something that would be nearly impossible to give up. It's staying put, but just to make sure, I'd better keep my eye on it…

What is something you possess that would be nearly impossible for you to give up?

Play video episode now.

You see a couple willing to do whatever it takes, even to go and seek the advice of a marriage counselor. Things seem to be working, they seem to be connecting. Then the counselor drops a bomb. There's silence in the room when they hear that if they want to have a stronger marriage, they need to downsize. "You need to have less money." You would have thought they were asked to cut off a limb or give away their child. Money has a way of doing that, stopping us in our tracks, even keeping us from something we really want.

What keeps James and Rebecca from having the kind of marriage they could have?

Why do you feel James and Rebecca were so unwilling to downsize?

¹⁷ As Jesus started to leave, a man ran to him and fell on his knees before Jesus. The man asked, "Good teacher, what must I do to have life forever?"

¹⁸ Jesus answered, "Why do you call me good? Only God is good. ¹⁹ You know the commands: 'You must not murder anyone. You must not be guilty of adultery. You must not steal. You must not tell lies about your neighbor. You must not cheat. Honor your father and mother.'

²⁰ The man said, "Teacher, I have obeyed all these things since I was a boy."

²¹ Jesus, looking at the man, loved him and said, "There is one more thing you need to do. Go and sell everything you have, and give the money to the poor, and you will have treasure in heaven. Then come and follow me."

²² He was very sad to hear Jesus say this, and he left sorrowfully, because he was rich.

²³ Then Jesus looked at his followers and said, "How hard it will be for the rich to enter the kingdom of God!"

²⁴ The followers were amazed at what Jesus said. But he said again, "My children, it is very hard to enter the kingdom of God! ²⁵ It is easier for a camel to go through the eye of a needle than for a rich person to enter the kingdom of God."

[26] The followers were even more surprised and said to each other, "Then who can be saved?"

[27] Jesus looked at them and said, "This is something people cannot do, but God can. God can do all things."

[28] Peter said to Jesus, "Look, we have left everything and followed you."

[29] Jesus said, "I tell you the truth, all those who have left houses, brothers, sisters, mother, father, children, or farms for me and for the Good News [30] will get more than they left. Here in this world they will have a hundred times more homes, brothers, sisters, mothers, children, and fields. And with those things, they will also suffer for their belief. But in the age that is coming they will have life forever. [31] Many who have the highest place now will have the lowest place in the future. And many who have the lowest place now will have the highest place in the future."

What do you learn about the rich man and Jesus?

What do you learn about the tension between wealth and following Jesus?

CULTURAL AND HISTORICAL THOUGHTS:

Mark 10:17–31 is part of Mark's "travel narrative" in which Jesus traveled from Galilee to Judea and its capital city of Jerusalem. In this section of the gospel, Jesus had left the familiar surroundings in his home-town of Capernaum on the Sea of Galilee and was now heading eighty miles south to Jerusalem.

This is the third teaching that we encounter as Jesus traveled southward to Jerusalem. First there was Jesus' teaching about marriage/divorce, then the blessings to be bestowed upon the children, and now his teaching about money/riches. In all three of his teachings, Jesus amazed his disciples, whose religious values and practices about marriage/divorce, children, and money had been shaped completely by the Old Testament and tradition.

Jesus was putting the rich young man (referred to as a "ruler" in Luke) to a test to see whether he personally and specifically loved God and his neighbor more than money. This test was similar to the story about Abraham in the Old Testament when God asked him to sacrifice his own son, Isaac. God was testing Abraham to see if Abraham loved God more than his son. Similarly, Jesus was testing this rich young man to see if he loved his riches more than God.

Jesus states, "It is easier for a camel to go through the eye of a needle than for a rich person to enter the kingdom of God" (v. 25). Biblical scholars conclude that this teaching is another example of Aramaic hyperbole (which they state the request Jesus made to sell "all" of his possessions was, also), overstatement, or exaggeration to a point. What was the point? The point is that it is very difficult (in fact, impossible without God) for a rich person to enter the kingdom of God. These scholars conclude that the "eye of the needle" was an Aramaic exaggeration that needs to be translated so that readers will understand that it was in the past and still is today very difficult for rich people to enter the kingdom of God because rich people tend to love their wealth more than God.

On the other hand, some students of the Bible conclude that there was actually a low gate by which camels could enter the city of Jerusalem and that low gate was called "the eye of the needle." Just as a camel needed to be "unburdened" or stripped of its baggage in order to squeeze through the small entry gate to the city, so a rich man needs to be stripped of his love of money in order to enter God's kingdom.

Playing professional baseball, I got this reaction all the time. Once people knew I was a Christian, they thought I was too soft, didn't have that edge, the little bit of nastiness that it took to win. They were wrong. I had both, but they just didn't think the two could coexist. Is money wrong? No, money can be great. God chooses to bless people differently—some with money, others with different things. I have the privilege of being around a lot of people who have a great balance. Sure, they have money—some even have lots of money—but they love Jesus. They haven't given up God to follow money. They have shown me that the two can coexist.

How do you see people struggling like the rich man today? How are they affected by these struggles?

How do these struggles impact people's ability to follow Jesus?

I watch *Deal or No Deal* with my kids whenever it's on. That show plays upon people's biggest desire, the need for something more. You can be satisfied with what you have, or you can risk it all for a bigger paycheck. People are banking on something that will meet all their needs, what they think will make all of their problems go away. The great question in the game is, do you take what the bank has to offer, or do you hold out for the million dollars? It's the same question Jesus asked the rich man. "Are you going to follow me, or are you going to go for the big bucks?" Essentially Jesus is looking at the young man and asking, "Deal or no deal?" The man answers, "No deal," and walks on. Sure, he might be set for this life, but what about the next?

In what ways in your life are you putting money before God? In what ways in your life are you putting God before money?

What courageous decision can you make in your life regarding money that would move you toward following God with all your heart?

Me? I don't have a God/money issue in my life. How could I if I don't have a lot of money in the first place? Well, I guess I do sometimes focus a lot on not having money. And now that I think about it, sometimes I kind of give God the "why don't you do something for me every once in a while" line. And when I don't feel like he does, God goes down a notch or two in my mind. I become a little more consumed with money, a little less dependent on God. I guess it doesn't really matter how much you have, it's easy to have a tension between God and money.

What are some of the reasons there is a tension between our desire for money and our desire to follow Christ? What are some reasons money seems to be such a big issue?

Were there times in your life when you chose money over God? What led to that decision? What was your life like?

Were there times when you chose God over money? What led to that decision? What was your life like?

If the opportunity arose to have a little more money and a little less Jesus, would you take it? Why or why not?

LEADER'S GUIDE

▄▄▄ NOTE TO LEADERS

As leaders, we have tried to make this experience as easy for you as possible. Don't try to do too much during your time together as a group—just ask and listen, and direct when necessary.

The questions have a flow, a progression, and are designed to get people talking. If you help the group start talking early on, they will continue to talk. You will notice that the questions start out easy and casual, creating a theme. The theme continues throughout the session, flowing through casual topics, then into world affairs, and then they begin getting personal.

When the questions ask about the Bible, spend time there. Dig in and scour the passage. Keep looking. You and your group will discover that looking into the Bible can be fun and interesting. Maybe you already know that, but there will be people in your group who don't—people who are afraid of their Bibles, or who don't think they can really study them.

Remember, we are seeking life change. This will happen by taking God's Word and applying it to your life, and to the lives of the people you are with. That's the goal for each person in the group. Fight for it.

▬ TIPS

So, are you a little nervous? Guess what—I get scared too. I always have a little apprehension when it comes to leading a group. It's what keeps me on my toes! Here are some things to keep in mind as you're preparing.

Think about your group. How does this week's topic relate to your group? Is this going to be an easy session? Is this going to be a challenge? The more at ease you are with the topic, the better the experience will be for your group.

Go over the leader's material early, and try to get to know the questions. Sometimes there are multiple questions provided at the end of the chapters. These are extra questions that can be used as supplemental questions at any point throughout the discussion. Look over these extra questions and see if any of them jump out at you. Don't feel that you have to address each question, but they are there if you need them. My worst nightmare is to be leading a group, and, with thirty minutes still left on the clock, we run out of questions and there's nothing left to talk about . . . so we sit there and stare at one another in painful silence.

Just remember to keep moving through all the questions. The most important goal of this study is to get personal and see how to apply biblical truths to your own life. When you're talking about how a passage plays out in the world today, a common mistake is to not take it deep enough . . . not to push the envelope and move it from what "they" should do to what "I" should do. As a leader, you will struggle with how much to push, how deep to dig. Sometimes it will be just right, sometimes you will push too hard, or sometimes not hard enough. Though it can be nerve-racking, it's the essence of being a leader.

Here are a few more tips:

- Get them talking, laughing, and having fun.
- Don't squelch emotion. Though it may tend to make you uncomfortable, to the point where you'll want to step in and rescue the moment, remember that leaders shouldn't always interfere.
- Jump in when needed. If the question is tough, make sure to model the answer. Try to be open about your own life. Often, the group will only go as deep as you are willing to go.
- When you look in the Bible for answers, don't quit too soon. Let people really search.
- Don't be afraid of silence.
- Lead the group—don't dominate it.

These are just a few things to think about before you begin.

▄▄▄ CHAPTER 1: INVESTMENTS

■ Growing up, what was your most important relationship?

Leader tip: If this is the first time you are meeting as a group, you might go ahead and answer this question first. Sometimes that makes it easier for others to answer. It also helps to model, on this first question, how long the answers should be. Typically you would want to keep answers to the first question on the shorter side, allowing for more time for the rest of the study. But if this is the first time you are meeting, you may want to go ahead and let them take a little longer with their answers.

You should always try to find the "why" in the first question. If someone just answers with a simple "my dad," follow up with another question like, "What was so special about your relationship with your dad?"

> **What do you learn about the master and each of the servants? What do the actions and responses of the master and each of the servants say about how they view their relationship with each other?**

Observations from the text:

The master: He's going away for a long time and trusts his servants enough to give them his money to handle for him. He knew each of his servants so well that he gave them an amount of money that was equivalent to their abilities. After divvying up his money to the servants, he left. He returned from the trip and called on his servants to give an account of what they did with what he entrusted them. Praised the two servants equally who invested the money. Told the two servants that he would give them more responsibilities due to their faithfulness and he wanted to celebrate with them. Was angry with the servant who hid the money and called him wicked and lazy. Told the third servant that he should have, at the very least, earned interest on the money. Ordered that the one bag of silver this servant had be taken away and distributed to the other servant who had doubled the money and now had ten bags already. Explained that those who do well with what they are given will be given even more so that they will have abundance. Also said that those who do nothing with the little they've been given will have it taken away. Threw the servant who didn't know or trust him into the outer darkness (where there would be weeping and gnashing of teeth).

Servant one (given five bags of silver) and **Servant two** (given two bags of silver): Invested and doubled the money. They approached the master first, anxious to give their account of what they had earned.

Servant three (given one bag of silver): Buried the money to hide it. Admitted his fear of the master, describing him as harsh and unfair. Was afraid he'd lose the money, so he hid it in the earth. Was satisfied with just returning the money to the master. He didn't know the master well enough to know what the reaction would be.

The relationships: The master entrusted each to their ability, which means he knew their abilities and had a trust level with each of them. The first and second servant felt like they knew the master—they wanted to please him and do well. The third servant didn't know the master well enough to trust him.

> God entrusts everyone with money and resources. What does faithful and unfaithful stewardship look like? How might that reflect a person's relationship with God?

Leader tip: Spend about five to seven minutes on this question. This question is designed to help your group understand what the parable means in today's culture and to make it more relevant in the lives of people today.

Leader note: You might want to think of people you know who seem to be faithful stewards with what God has given them. Do they spend more than they have, leading to large debts? Do they handle their money and their lives with humble and grateful attitudes? Think about the relationship you think they have with God. Do they correlate?

> **How does your relationship with God affect the ways you use the money and resources God has given you? What relational changes will you make to help improve your stewardship?**

Leader tip: Spend about seven to ten minutes on this question. You may want to answer this question first, which should help the rest of the group open up. There are a couple of things people don't like talking about much, and one of them is how they handle their money. So be prepared for silence. And remember, it's OK to call on people if they don't volunteer.

Leader note: It may be helpful to consider other resources than just money. Maybe make a list of resources that you have available—your home (which could be opened up for Bible studies, visiting missionaries, and other kingdom-building types of activities), your car (shuttling people to and from church), your cooking or building skills (making dishes for church events or helping build houses for less fortunate people), etc.

Commentary: In relational changes you are really talking about feeling close to God—knowing him and living for him. There are many ways to make this happen. The question is, how will you make that happen? Does that mean spending more quiet time with him? Do you need to get into a Bible study class? How is your prayer life? What about the relationships you are in?

■ CHAPTER 2: STUFF

■ **For you, what are the most important aspects of a satisfying relationship?**

Leader tip: Spend about five minutes on this question.

Leader note: A recent survey showed an overwhelming percentage of people (95 percent) put trust as the aspect that was most important to a satisfying relationship.

Leader tip: If everyone throws trust out as their answer, you might want to ask the "why" question. Why is trust so important?

■ **What were the man in the crowd and the man with the barns concerned about? What was Jesus' response, and what were his concerns for them?**

Leader tip: Spend about seven to ten minutes on this question. This passage contains a parable about greed as well as a warning about worrying about provision. Since the first part of this question focuses on the parable, read through verses 13–21 first and answer the first question. Then proceed to the rest of the verses and answer the second question.

Leader note: It might be kind of interesting to let your group know that when the man from the crowd called out to him, Jesus had been teaching about important topics like unbelief and hypocrisy in the church and among its leaders. This shows the heart of the man in the crowd.

Observations from the text: Both men were concerned with their money and possessions. They were worried about whether they would have enough, and trusted only in an inheritance or hoarding and preserving a bountiful harvest. They were selfish, greedy, seeking abundance for themselves, not sharing, not taking what they needed, but wanting more.

Jesus responded that life is not measured by what is accumulated. Jesus said that a person is a fool to store up earthly wealth and not have a relationship with God. Jesus wanted the crowd to know that the relationship with the Provider is the most important thing, so he used a story about money and possessions. Jesus warned that life is more than food, your body, and clothing. He explained that God provides for even the grass, birds, and flowers—God takes care of them and they don't worry about it for even one minute. He wants the crowd to remember to trust God since he wants to provide for them. He tells them to sell their possessions and give to the poor. He says that the treasures stored up from generosity instead of from greed, worry, and anxiety over money will be eternal.

If there were a scale of trust with money on one side and God on the other, where would you put the two men in the story?

Money ——|———|———|———|———|———|———|———|———|—— God

Leader tip: Take about ten minutes on this question, along with the next two.

Leader tip: You may want to have a large whiteboard or flip chart and draw out the scale for a visual for your group.

Commentary: Both the man with the inheritance who wanted it divided differently and the man who stored up his bountiful harvest were putting their trust in money. The man who came to Jesus for a different accounting of the inheritance may be showing that he trusted God a little, in that he was looking to a godly man for the answers, but in reality, his question showed where his heart was.

What might move them in one direction or the other?

Commentary: If either man would have recognized that their bounty was from God in the first place, they would have been more grateful and content. They also would have trusted him to continue to provide and instead wouldn't have had to be greedy in renegotiating an inheritance or hoarding the harvest.

■ What are the consequences of putting trust in money? In God?

Commentary: The consequences of putting trust in money are always negative. First of all, there is never satisfaction. Someone who trusts money is always anxious about having enough, even if they are wealthy. Will this last? Will next year be as plentiful as this year? Trusting in money can also lead to prideful behavior—*look at what **I've** done!* It can lead to greed, which destroys relationships with families, with co-workers, and with God. Trusting in money is a fool's game because money will never provide for anyone beyond their years on this earth.

On the other hand, complete trust in God for provision gives a sense of peace, as well as a spirit of gratefulness and thankfulness. It will provide for eternity.

■ Using the scale below, where would you place yourself? How will your mind-set and actions have to change to move you closer to God?

Money ┼──┼──┼──┼──┼──┼──┼──┼──┼── God

Leader tip: Spend about ten minutes on these last two questions.

Leader tip: You might want to have everyone draw the scale of trust on a piece of paper and put a mark where they would place themselves. Then tell them to revisit this mark next week and see if they've made any progress toward trusting God more.

Leader note: An easy way to check how much trust is placed in money is to imagine that all of your investments are gone, and there is no money left in your savings or checking accounts. It is the end of the month, and everything is due tomorrow. What level of anxiety are you feeling? Is it fear? Or is there peace that everything will be OK? Now think about the scale of trust.

Commentary: Sometimes the thinking that needs to change is caused by a look back at difficult times when God has provided. Maybe members of your group would benefit from taking a minute and thinking about all of the times God has come through with food, with clothes, with money for medicine, or whatever the need was. The provision might have come from church members, or neighbors, or other people doing the work of the Lord. Have them consider those times and then commit to trusting God more.

■ **What will be the good and bad consequences of making that change?**

Leader note: In an opposite exercise from above, have your group imagine that there is plenty of money in the account to pay all of their bills. Imagine that they even have some left over to give to someone in need. Is there a sense of calm? Is there a sense of joy at the thought of blessing others? Remind your group that this is what God promises when we trust in him instead of trusting in money.

CHAPTER 3: LEVERAGE

What was the first expensive thing you ever owned?

Leader tip: Spend about five minutes on this opening question. You want people to recount what it felt like to save up for something and then how it felt to be able to buy or invest in something.

Leader note: Coach your group to think of things in their childhood, or maybe it was a college education—either for themselves or one of their kids. It could be a car or a house. If your group throws out one-word answers, you can always ask a follow-up. For example, if they answer "a car," you can ask, "What kind of car and how long did you save up for it?"

What did the rich man and the manager want, and what did they do to get it? What did Jesus want the disciples to learn from the story?

Leader tip: Spend five to seven minutes on this question. Parables are sometimes a little harder to understand than direct teaching. It might help to read the whole passage first, then ask the question and then look at the passage again.

Leader note: *Mammon* is defined as material wealth or possessions especially those having a debasing influence.

Observations from the text: The rich man wanted his affairs handled for him. He wanted a full accounting from the servants who handled the money.

The manager wanted to make sure he would be taken care of after he lost his job. He tried to win friends by cutting their debts owed to the rich man, hoping they would reward him by helping him when he was down and out. He acted shrewdly in his position.

Jesus wanted the disciples to learn to use their money and resources shrewdly, influencing people for eternal benefit. This way, even when they lose all of their money, the people whom they have influenced will welcome them into heaven. See verse 9: "Use your worldly resources to benefit others and make friends. Then, when your earthly possessions are gone, they will welcome you to an eternal home."

■ **What are ways people use money today to gain friends and influence people?**

Leader tip: Spend about ten minutes on this question and the next.

Commentary: People use their money for influencing others all the time. Consider politics: thousand-dollar-per-plate dinners just so the politicians can have the ear of someone who might make decisions regarding their interests. Sometimes people use their money to donate to buildings and schools to get something named after them. You see people inviting people of power to nice dinners, hoping for reciprocation in favors.

■ **In the same way, how do people use their resources to produce eternal benefits?**

Commentary: Some of these same activities would have different outcomes if the motivations were different. For instance, the political dinners could still be advantageous if the politician were lobbying to change school curriculum in order to teach creation, alongside evolution. Or if the person donating money to a building project honestly wanted to help people by building hospitals, schools, or low-income housing instead of just publicizing his or her own name.

■ **What are some direct and creative ways you can use your money to not just make friends, but point people to God?**

Leader tip: Spend about seven to ten minutes on this last question.

Leader note: Look at the answers you came up with earlier. Take them a level deeper by having your group members claim one of the ways to influence friends for eternal purposes. It might mean just putting a name to the person they are going to take to dinner, or commit to championing a good work that will have lasting effects. Maybe you just need to take a neighbor who is searching for answers to a sporting event so you can get the opportunity to talk about things.

The point is that we have to keep our priorities straight. Wealth is to be used, not served. The truth about money is that we can either be stewards of it or we can be servants of it.

▰▰ CHAPTER 4: CHARITY

▰ Describe a time when someone was over-the-top generous to you.

Leader tip: Spend about five minutes on this first question.

Leader note: Model how long the answers should be. You want your group to be able to describe whatever generosity they are going to talk about, but you want to make sure you have enough time for the rest of the questions.

What do you learn about the cause and effect of giving: for God, the giver, and the receiver?

Leader tip: Spend about five to seven minutes on this question.

Leader note: One way to go through this question is to first look at the cause and effect of giving for God, then the giver, and then the receiver—that way you are going through the passage three times. Or you can go through and look at the cause and effect for each component all at once, as we have below.

Observations from the text: Few seeds = small crop; generous amount of seeds = generous crop. Each person's giving is determined by their own heart; there is no "set" amount. Giving should be done willingly and cheerfully because God loves cheerful giving. God provides generously—all that is needed, enough to have plenty left over to share. Giving generously to the poor will result in the good deeds being remembered forever. God provides the seed to grow the wheat and the bread to eat. God will also provide the resources for giving generously. God enriches people so they can give generously. Generosity leads to people giving thanks to God. Generous giving results in two things—needs being met and joyful thanks to God. God will receive glory. Generosity proves obedience to Jesus. Recipients of generosity will pray with deep affection for the givers because of the overflowing grace God has given. The gift from God is too wonderful for words.

What are some of the ways the world views giving? What are ways that Christians view giving? Compare and contrast your answers.

Leader tip: Spend about ten minutes on these questions.

Commentary: Many times the world views giving in a reserved manner. If people give, they still want to be sure to have enough left over for their own needs. Or sometimes they view those to whom they are giving as undeserving of the gift, and thankless toward the giver. Or that if you give you should do it to get something back—tax deductions, notoriety, paybacks, and favors. A common Christian view is one of tithing a straight 10 percent. Some Christians view giving as a sacrificial act and give generously. Still other Christians view giving in the same way as unbelievers do.

How do the views align or differ from the truths of the passage we just read?

Leader note: The truths of the passage reveal that the more you give, the more God gives you to give! Also, that the receivers will be thankful and will give God praise and thanks. God will be glorified!

What principles from the passage have changed your view on giving? How may these principles influence your giving in the future?

Leader tip: Spend about ten minutes on these last two questions.

Leader note: This passage is convicting in that it promises that if people give, God will provide for everything they need. It may be surprising to your group that the more they give, the more they receive from God. Or that this extra they receive from God is intended to be more to give away! They may be encouraged that God will be glorified in their giving or that the recipients of their generosity will in turn pray affectionately for them.

What is an area in your life where you feel called to give? What is a step you can take to give in this area?

Leader note: Have your group consider the needs of their families, community, church, and the world as a whole. There are so many opportunities to spread generosity.

CHAPTER 5: PRIORITIES

What is something you possess that would be nearly impossible for you to give up?

Leader tip: Spend about five minutes on this question.

■ What do you learn about the rich man and Jesus?

Observations from the text: The young man was looking for a way to get to heaven and came to Jesus figuring he could get the answer he needed. He had worked to keep the commandments all of his life. He was very wealthy and couldn't give up his wealth to the poor and follow Jesus, even if it meant he could get into heaven. He was sad after he realized that he couldn't do what it took to receive eternal life.

Jesus knew that the man was wealthy and told him he had to give everything to the poor in order to get into heaven. He told him there would be treasure in heaven waiting for him. He told the man to follow him after giving up his riches. Jesus then told his amazed disciples that it is harder for a camel to go through the eye of a needle than for a rich man to enter heaven. When the disciples looked at him incredulously, Jesus reminded them that although it is impossible for man to take a camel through the eye of the needle (and for a wealthy man to enter heaven), all things are possible with God. Jesus also told his disciples that those who left everything to follow him would receive one hundred times whatever they left behind. They would also receive eternal life. He also made the statement that those who are greatest in this lifetime would be least important in eternity, and those who *seem* least important now *will be* the greatest then.

■ What do you learn about the tension between wealth and following Jesus?

Leader note: Jesus says the tension is so great that without God it is impossible for a wealthy person to enter heaven. That statement shows that the more wealth a person has, the harder it is to give it up. The tension between God and money grows with the amount of wealth. Jesus' last statement in verse 31 ties perceived importance or the desire to be important to this passage. It shows that wealth is tied with pride, which again causes tension in following Jesus. Those who use their wealth to serve or give to the poor and needy would not be prideful and would therefore have less standing in their way to follow Christ.

■ How do you see people struggling like the rich man today? How are they affected by these struggles?

Leader tip: Spend ten minutes on these two questions.

Leader note: Your group may have specific examples of this—remind them to withhold names, even if it is a family member.

Commentary: People tend to let their wealth determine their worth, to the point that giving up anything, let alone everything, would be impossible. Sometimes wealthy people are genuinely seeking Jesus, but more likely than not, if they were told that money was in the way of their relationship with him, they would be tempted to choose money over him. Look at the results of people who live their lives clinging to their bank accounts, stocks, and possessions, and drive home the point of how unfulfilling that lifestyle is.

■ **How do these struggles impact people's ability to follow Jesus?**

Leader note: It seems as though the more people have, the harder it is to consider giving it all up. If you asked people in the poorest neighborhood to give up everything in their bank accounts in order to have eternal life, what would be their response? What about asking people in the wealthiest section of town to do the same thing? What would be their response?

■ **In what ways in your life are you putting money before God? In what ways in your life are you putting God before money?**

Leader tip: Spend several minutes on these last questions.

Leader note: Have your group consider how much time in a day is consumed with thinking about money, versus how much time is spent on their relationship with Jesus. If they were faced with a business deal or a Bible study, which would they choose? Have them place themselves in the parable you are studying. What would be their response when Jesus said, "Go and sell everything you have, and give the money to the poor, and you will have treasure in heaven. Then come and follow me."

What courageous decision can you make in your life regarding money that would move you toward following God with all your heart?

Leader note: Try to get your group to commit to one thing they can do that will decrease the tension between money and their relationship with God. Is it getting rid of worry? Stop hoarding too much? Letting go of anxiety about about having enough to provide for themselves and their families? How can they take their concerns to God and ask for his help in this endeavor?

LIQUID would love to thank:

Chris Marcus, for being a producer, designer, editor, and director of photography on the project. You did it all, and we could not have done it without you.

Mariners Church: To the staff and small group department for all of their help and insight into this entire project. And to the congregation and elder board for their prayers and support.

Kenton Beshore, for the beauty of flow questions.

All of the incredible people in North Carolina, who got this whole thing started.

The cast and crew, for the endless hours of hard work and incredible performances.

Aaron and Mark of Tank Creative, for making us sound good.

Chris Ferebee of Yates and Yates for all of his guidance and direction.

Cindy Western, for her help in crafting great questions.

Pastor Bruce Nelson and the Mariners Church Stewardship Ministry, for all of their support and insight into the production of *Money Talks*.

Our incredible editor, Kim Hearon, who, to put it simply, had to deal with us. You made it fun.

All the people at Thomas Nelson, for your hard work and expertise.

And we thank God for having his hand on this project and blessing it.